THE *NEW* IDIOT-PROOF GUIDE TO CUSTOMER LOYALTY

JOE HEUER

joespeaks.com

The *NEW* Idiot-Proof Guide to Customer Loyalty

Copyright © 2007 by Joe Heuer

Published by Daffynitions Press
Glendale, Wisconsin

Published and distributed in the United States by:

Daffynitions Press
2435 West Greenwood Road
Glendale, Wisconsin 53209
(414) 247-0936
(800) 492-3548

Library of Congress Control Number: 2007904952
ISBN: 978-0-9647618-7-2

Cover and layout by Hausch Design Agency, Milwaukee, Wisconsin hauschdesign.com

HAUSCH DESIGN AGENCY

Also by Joe Heuer

- *Business Daffynitions: Humor from the Workplace*
- *The Wit and Wisdom of a Regular Joe*
- *The Pocket Guide to Patient Loyalty*

Dedication

To my wonderfully loving family, who treat my weirdness as if it's the most natural thing in the world. Lisa, you are the love of my life. Rachel & Alexandra, you bring me a joy I could never have imagined possible.

Acknowledgments

If it were not for all the pathetic excuses for customer service out there, I would not have any idea what leads to customer loyalty or what goes into truly exceptional service. Never in my wildest dreams would I have imagined that I'd be thanking all those people who have delivered all the incredibly awful service that I have experienced.

Without you (and you know who you are) this book would not have been possible. Thank you…and keep up the mediocre work.

Why I Wrote This Book

I wrote this book for three reasons. First, I have a sincere desire to help organizations make the quantum leap from customer satisfaction to customer loyalty. Second, I am sick and tired of all the crappy service that I have received. Third, it's fun and my philosophy is that if you always do fun things, there will always be plenty of fun things to do.

Here are a couple of customer service experiences that I encountered on the same day that pushed me over the edge and inspired me to write the book.

A while back I observed the following exchange in one of those home remodeling big box stores:

Customer: "Can you please tell me where the wallpaper is?"

Service representative (while rolling his eyes in disgust): "It's under the sign that says wallpaper, lady."

Both the customer and I laughed out loud as the poor-excuse-for-a-service-representative just turned and walked away shaking his head.

Then it got absolutely hilarious. Later that day I called with a complaint about my cell phone. I won't mention the particular company, although suffice it to say their customer service was hideous and I had to speak with five different representatives to get a simple problem straightened out.

The comical part of the encounter came after I explained to service representative number five what I had been told moments earlier by service representative number four. Keep in mind that she was speaking about a coworker:

"Whoever you spoke to must have been on drugs. They're sure hiring some real idiots around here lately and I'm getting sick and tired of having to clean up their messes. I'd suggest you try to get out of your contract and find another provider cause things are getting really bad around here." Needless to say, I did.

Here's the crown jewel from a recent experience at the world's second busiest airport. After spending twelve hours traveling and then standing in line for nearly an hour when my luggage failed to appear on the carousel, I stood face to face with an airline customer service representative. When I told her that my luggage had not arrived she asked, "Sir, has your plane landed?" Now that's a special kind of stupid!

As Frank Zappa said, "It's not getting any smarter out there. You have to come to terms with stupidity and make it work for you."

I used to be disgusted but now I try to be amused. That's my new stance on lousy customer service, since it's a whole lot more fun to go through life amused. Additionally, the pathetic service out there provides excellent illustrations of what to avoid doing if your goal is to create customer loyalty.

A Note from Joe

This is not intended to be a motivational book, so if you are motivated after reading it don't you dare blame me!

I am not a motivational speaker. Motivational speakers are the professional wrestlers of the corporate world.

The truth is that nobody can motivate you but you. And motivation is more than simply having a healthier defeatist attitude than your coworkers.

My intent is to give you a creative whack upside the head so that you will now think about customer loyalty in a leading-edge manner.

Believe it if you need it...if you don't just pass it on.

Customer Loyalty from A-Z (sort of)

I was going to do a little A-Z guide to Customer Loyalty, but I decided against it for three reasons:

1. I just couldn't commit to the linear thinking required to follow that particular bouncing ball. (How's that for a paradox?)

2. That whole alphabetization thing is way too complicated.

3. I couldn't think of anything good for X, Y or Z. Either that or by the time I got to the end of the alphabet I had already used up all the words I've mastered.

Therefore, I've decided to share these universal principles for creating customer loyalty in no particular order.

I know, I know…your industry is unique. You have different challenges and problems. It doesn't matter. These principles are universal. They apply to any industry, including yours.

Customers: people you better start treating a whole lot better because they currently possess your future fortune.

What is Customer Loyalty?

I figured I'd better put this section at the beginning so we all share a common understanding of what specifically we're talking about here. Let's begin with a brief definition of our terms.

What is a customer? First, for our purposes the terms customer, client, patient and member are interchangeable. They each refer to someone who wants or needs something you have to offer and are willing to pay for it. Whether you are talking about a product, service or information, the bottom line is that customers are people who want to give you money as a means of exchange for whatever you have that they would like to have.

What is loyalty? I regularly ask audiences to answer that question in one word. The responses I hear most often are commitment, responsiveness, great service, repeat business (okay, so some people don't quite get the concept of one word), dedication and excellence. Those are all certainly components of customer loyalty, but none of them answer the question.

In one word, loyalty is a feeling or an emotion. Make a special note of this because we will be coming back to this concept repeatedly.

Putting the two together, customer loyalty is a feeling that people have about you that inspires them to give you money. It is a feeling that motivates them to encourage their friends and family to give you money as well. Loyal customers do both of these things, and not necessarily because of the quality of your product or services. They do it because of how they feel when they think about their experiences dealing with you.

Loyal customers would rather fight than switch. (Yes, you are really old if you remember where that phrase came from.) Not only do they keep coming back to give you more money, but truly loyal customers become your most effective sales force. They tell the world how great you are, and that is worth more than any advertising or marketing campaign you can undertake.

Create enough loyal customers and they will be the only sales force you will ever need. Eventually, you will be able to eliminate your entire marketing department.

Note to marketing people: Lighten up! That was a joke.

Loyalty will lead to action on the part or your customers. And that action will result in putting more food on your table and a bigger roof in an exclusive neighborhood over your head.

"People will forget
what you said,
People will forget
what you did,
But people will
never forget how
you made
them feel."

Maya Angelou

Loyalty implies a powerful relationship. Create that bond by making people feel that their lives are somehow better for having dealt with you. You gotta show them how much you care, not just tell them in a cutesy worthless brochure!

Customer Satisfaction Means Nothing!

Before we go any further, I need to address one more group of people you have heard so much about. They are the satisfied customers. These people are not the same as loyal customers. Most satisfied customers are not really satisfied at all. They are usually just habitual customers who frequent certain companies only because it's convenient. For example, they shop there because it's on the way home from work or near the kids' school.

Satisfied is a customer service term meaning excessively mediocre. People who consider themselves satisfied customer report that they will leave to go somewhere else in a heartbeat. If they can get a similar product or service for seven cents cheaper or half-a-mile closer to home, they will say adios in an instant.

Consequently, customer satisfaction is a pathetic goal. Banish the term from your vocabulary right now!

Loyal customers, on the other hand, will keep coming back even if it is a little less convenient and a little more expensive.

"Service is the rent we pay for living on this planet. It is the very purpose of life and not something you do in your spare time."

Marian Wright Edelman

Customer Service is NOT Rocket Science!

One Monday morning when my beautiful little girls were three years old, they asked me where I was going and for one of the few times in my life I was speechless. I wasn't about to tell a pair of three-year-olds that I would be out delivering customer service training. They were already at the age where they started looking at me like I was nuts, and I didn't really want to add fuel to that particular fire.

As I sat thinking about how to respond, I realized that if I couldn't explain it to them in a way they would understand, maybe I didn't have a very good grasp on it myself.

Suddenly, I had a BFO (Blinding Flash of the Obvious). I've got several 300-page books on customer service sitting on my bookshelves, and I've even read the first chapter of most of them...but it doesn't take three hundred pages to explain customer service. In that moment I realized that everything we need to know about customer service we learned in kindergarten.

Here's the BFO part. Customer service is two simple principles:

1. **Be nice**
2. **Be helpful**

That's it. When you break customer service down to its essence, that's all there really is. Most kindergartners have mastered these two concepts, while most companies run by adults seem to have no clue what that means.

If you are seeking a more complicated explanation of customer service then this probably isn't the right book for you. There is plenty of boring information out there that could better suit your needs. However, if you are genuinely interested in the simple truths that will earn customer loyalty (along with a healthy dose of irreverence and sarcasm), keep reading. This book can help you create your own hugely profitable road map to customer loyalty.

Everything you need to know about customer service you learned in kindergarten:

1. Be Nice
2. Be Helpful

Duh!

The Current State of Customer Service

I recently asked a gentleman sitting next to me on an airplane what he thought about customer service, and his deadpan response made me laugh out loud. "I think it would be a good idea," he said.

Take a moment to think about the level of service you typically receive out there in the vast wasteland of what only nominally passes for customer service. Begin paying attention to the places where you spend your money. How do they treat you? Are people nice? Are they helpful?

If you are like most people, you're starting to get pissed off just thinking about it. I know what you're thinking and you are right...it is absolutely pathetic out there. Generally speaking, customer service in our country sucks! Yes, you read that correctly...**customer service at most businesses sucks more than your vacuum cleaner!** Obviously, I've decided not to sugarcoat it.

While this is a real drag for us as customers, the flip side is that if we learn from these experiences they can help us develop our own brand of kick-ass service that will earn customer loyalty.

Nothing in this book is complicated. It is simple, although not always easy. It does, however, require you to take action. And that's a small price to pay for customer loyalty.

I've Just Gotta Rant

Once, just once, when I call a company to tell them their lemon of a product broke down after just three days, I'd like to hear the underpaid, untrained drone on the other end of the line apologize, accept responsibility for making it right and ship me out another Veg-o-Matic the same day. Is this really too much to ask?

The next time you hear a company proclaiming their renewed commitment to customer service, here is what they are really saying, "If you think our customer service is lousy now, you should have seen us before!"

Customer service, as well as plain-old common courtesy, has gone the way of the rotary phone. Between the pathetic indifference and the we're-doing-you-a-favor attitude, you have a better chance of winning the lottery than you do of finding someone out there who can actually help solve your problems. Okay, maybe I'm exaggerating a little bit, but not much.

I'm always appalled when I enter a place of business without being greeted, where employees not only lack the habit of common courtesy, they act as if I'm infringing on their time. Then when they do finally approach me it's clear that they would rather be doing anything else besides helping me. It makes me just want to rush right back there and give them more money. And tell my friends about the experience, too.

Employees in most organizations tend to be unclear on the concept of who actually pays their salaries. They seem to think the companies they work for are responsible for providing the paychecks. That is wrong on so many levels. It is the customers, the people walking through your doors every day, who are responsible for making certain that you get paid. That should be all the motivation you will ever need to treat them like gold!

In a survey done by Public Agenda, nearly half the people who responded reported that they had walked out of a store in the past year because of poor customer service. I know I have.

If you really want to feel like you are imposing on people, walk into a department store fifteen minutes before closing time. The clerks who have congregated around the register will immediately look at their watches and then roll their eyes in a synchronized display of apathy before giving you the fake customer service smile.

Customer service incompetence is astonishing, yet it doesn't have to be that way. Let's get real...how complicated is it to be nice and be helpful?

The problem is that the prevailing philosophy that passes for customer service seems to be to take the lowest-paid, least-trained employees and put them on the front lines to see how much they can irritate the people who are responsible for putting money in the shareholders' pockets. That might not be quite so bad if they at least had the authority to solve customers' problems.

In this era of cost-cutting measures, does it really make sense to pinch pennies when it comes to the employees who have the most direct contact with your customers? After all, the customers are your real bosses.

We are a service-starved society. That is why the companies that provide phenomenal service have legions of loyal customers. Phenomenal service makes us feel great. Oh, have I mentioned that customer loyalty is about *feelings*

If you really care about your customers, stop putting your lowest-paid, least-trained employees on the front lines of customer service!

What's the Solution?

Here's a radical idea. Train employees to provide exemplary service and then reward them when they do. How complicated is that?

Of course, training is effective only if the people in senior management are modeling the proper behavior. All the training in the world is not going to significantly raise your customer service levels if the top dogs are treating their own people poorly. If they expect everyone else to do it, senior management has got to walk the walk instead of just paying lip service to the talk. When the people at the top of an organization commit not only resources, but also their own time and energy to customer service, the likelihood of creating customer loyalty increases exponentially.

Here is the key. Treat people the way *they* want to be treated, make them feel good about the experience and you will create life-long loyal customers. These people will both seek out opportunities to give you money and encourage others to do so. What more could you ask for?

Service is the lifeblood of your organization. I'd be willing to bet that if you line your brochure up next to the brochures of your competitors, there is not a whole lot of difference in what you are offering. How you provide those products and services will determine whether or not you earn customer loyalty.

How much simpler can it get? Earn people's loyalty by delivering kick-ass service. Be proactive. Do a little something extra, and make their experiences dealing with you memorable. Serve your customers better than anyone else does—it's the only thing in the loyalty equation that is totally under your control.

These are the simple steps that will help you make the quantum leap to true service excellence. Unfortunately, true service excellence is extremely rare. Many companies claim that it is a priority, but very few of them actually walk the talk.

Following are some more idiot-proof solutions that anyone can implement to provide the service excellence that leads to customer loyalty.

"You have brains in your head and feet in your shoes. You can steer yourself any direction you choose."

Dr. Seuss

What do you want your customers to think, feel and say about their experiences with you?

A Lesson from Caddyshack

There is a fabulous lesson regarding perspective in the classic movie Caddyshack. Carl, a character played by Bill Murray, was the assistant groundskeeper on a golf course. He was trying, without much success, to catch a gopher that was tearing up the course. In a brilliantly profound BFO (Blinding Flash of the Obvious) he realized that if he wanted to catch the gopher, he had to think like a gopher.

While I am not suggesting that you think of your customers as gophers, there was a method to his madness that is relevant to you. If your goal is to create loyal customers, then start to think like a customer. In other words, put yourself in their shoes.

For example, how do you feel when you are forced to navigate a complicated voice mail system, which is the device of choice for organizations that want to annoy their customers without making the effort to do so live and in person. If you find it annoying, take that as a cue as to what your customers think about it!

Learn to think about the service you provide from the customer's perspective and you will be well on your way to creating the positive relationships that lead to customer loyalty.

Where Are You Loyal?

Now take a moment to think about a company where you are truly loyal. What have they done to make you loyal? How do they treat you? Moreover, how do they make you *feel*? If you can't think of a specific company, simply imagine what it would be like to be loyal and then answer these questions.

Remember that success leaves clues. Use your answers to these questions as you begin creating your own roadmap to earning customer loyalty.

Don't feel bad if you can't think of any company where you are loyal. It is common in my presentations for fewer than ten percent of the attendees to be able to identify even one company to whom they are loyal. That is just more validation of my premise that service levels have reached a new high in lows.

If you were put on trial for earning customer loyalty, would a jury have enough evidence to convict you?

The Psychology of Customer Loyalty
(The abbreviated Idiot-proof version)

Human beings are, first and foremost, creatures of emotion. We make the majority of our decisions based on our feelings or emotions. We then attempt to justify those decisions logically. When we are deciding with whom to do business, that decision is almost always based on our feelings.

Obviously, making people feel good about doing business with you is the heart of the matter. In other words, the heart of the matter really is the heart of the matter.

Are you starting to notice a pattern here?

"When dealing
with people,
remember you are
not dealing with
creatures of logic,
but with creatures
of emotion."

Dale Carnegie

The WOW! Factor

The quickest idiot-proof path to customer loyalty is to find a way to make your customers say WOW or it's first cousin, COOL! Go above and beyond the call of duty. Give them a benefit they don't even know exists. If they forgot their coupon, give them the I-forgot-my-coupon discount. Use your creativity to turn the ordinary into the extraordinary.

Here is a WOW story for the ages. A colleague of mine was getting her hair done the day before her mother's funeral. She happened to mention in passing that she was disappointed about how her mother's hair looked in the casket. The next day when she arrived at the funeral parlor, she was surprised to see that someone had cut and styled her mother's hair beautifully. Her stylist, after hearing about my colleague's disappointment, had gone to the funeral parlor later that day and remedied the situation. WOW!!!

What can you do right now to make the experience of doing business with you so memorable that your customers will say WOW?

The key to earning
loyalty is to deliver
the kick-ass service
that will make
your customers say
WOW
or its first cousin,
COOL!

Creating Memorable Experiences

How are you creating the memorable experiences that lead to customer loyalty? Every employee in your company should be able to answer this question off the top of their head, because customer experience is where loyalty is earned or lost.

Why do you think Victoria's Secret can sell the same underwear and lingerie for five times the price that other stores charge? They have created a positive experience by pampering women and making men feel comfortable purchasing women's undergarments.

My local Starbucks creates an experience that compels me to drive past several other coffee shops to visit them. They make me feel like I'm on the old sitcom *Cheers*. No matter how busy they are, whenever I walk into the store, Vicky, the manager, shouts out my name to welcome me. I have also noticed that each morning they greet a large percentage of their customers by name. Vicky and her staff are always having fun and they truly embody the principle of creating fun experiences for their customers.

Contrast that with my recent experience at a local appliance store. I went in to return a clock radio that my wife received as a gift. Unfortunately, it did not have the features that Lisa wanted. The store refused to take it back, citing their fifteen-day return policy.

While the customer service manager feebly and unapologetically explained their pathetic policy, I noticed two signs on a bulletin board that urged employees to *Wow the Customer* and *Make the Customer's Experience Memorable*. What a joke! They couldn't have cared less about my experience.

In the end, they lost thousands of dollars in future business over the stupidity of their policies and a simple $47.30 return. They did, however, create a memorable experience. I remember walking away thinking *Wow, their customer service really sucks*!

Which type of memorable experiences are you creating for your customers?

The Mantra

Customer loyalty begins with me!

This must become the mantra of every person in your organization, from the CEO to the mail clerk, if you intend to create customer loyalty!

What's in it for ME?

What's in it for me? That is the number one question most of us ask ourselves on a consistent basis. Why should I be so concerned with providing the top-notch service that leads to customer loyalty?

The explanation is elementary, Watson. First, you can't expect to further your own career unless you learn to deliver tremendous service. Second, phenomenal service is always noticed, and you never know who is doing the noticing. It might be someone in your own company who can suggest you for a promotion, or an external customer who can offer you a better job at another company.

If nothing else, providing fantastic service will lead to the sense of inner fulfillment that can only come from knowing that you have helped another person.

That is what's in it for you.

"I slept, and I dreamt that life was all joy.
I woke and saw that life was
but service.
I served and discovered that service was joy."

Rabindrath Tagore

Beware the Process Geeks

We have already established that customer service is a simple concept. Be vigilant in keeping it that way, because the process geeks in your organization will do their best to complicate it as much as humanly possible.

If you are not sure who the process geeks are, they are the people who always want to do seven more case studies, pilot programs and reengineering on matters as basic as how you answer the phone. They are usually so wrapped up in systems that they're completely oblivious to the immense impact of the human interaction. Watch out for the process geeks at all costs. They are often a bigger threat to customer service than most consultants, primarily because they don't go away after three weeks.

If your goal is to create loyal

customers, remember:

PEOPLE COME FIRST!

Tasks are a distant second.

Always!

The Simplicity of Service

"Everybody can be great…because anybody can serve. You don't have to have a college degree to serve. You don't have to make the subject and verb agree to serve…you only need a heart full of grace, a soul generated by love."

Martin Luther King, Jr. said that. It does not matter that he wasn't speaking specifically about customer service. What matters is the essence of this simple message:
Everyone can serve.

The Customer Loyalty Creed

Do exactly what you say you are going to do

When you say you are going to do it

The way you promised to do it

And then do a little something extra

The Trying Syndrome

Beware the trying syndrome. When someone tells you they will *try* to do something, isn't it usually a safe bet that it is not going to happen?

Trying is a loud exhibition of effort, lacking only in results. Either commit to doing what it takes to delight your customers or don't waste your time and theirs. How annoying is it when a company tells you they will try to have something done by a certain time and then fails to come through?

Do what you say you are going to do, when you say you are going to do it or you will lose credibility in the eyes of your customers. It's not always easy, but it is simple. Can you afford to lose credibility with your customers?

Trying is a whining word that people use to make excuses for why they do not keep their commitments. Banish it from your vocabulary right now, or at least catch yourself the next time you hear it coming out of your mouth. Simply stop and restate what you are committed to doing.

If trying was the secret to success, then Harold Stassen would have been elected president of the United States at least twice!

Treat Every Customer as if They Were Your Grandma

Treat every customer as if they were your own grandma. Would this alter the way you serve?

Recently, the human resources director at one company stopped me during a training to ask for clarification regarding whether I was talking about his maternal or paternal grandma. This person was obviously unclear on the concept. At that moment I knew it was going to be a long day.

Typically, when I ask this question people answer yes. When I ask why, the standard response is because they love their grandma. While it is nice to hear that people love their grandmas, doesn't every human being you encounter deserve the same care, courtesy, compassion, appreciation, understanding, respect and attention that you would give to your grandma?

If you do not already treat customers this way, give it a shot. If it doesn't work out you can always go back to the way you have always done things.

Treating Customers as Guests
(An addendum to treating every customer as if they were your grandma)

What would happen if you adopted the philosophy of treating your customers like guests? Do you think it would increase your chances of earning their loyalty?

You do not have to be in the hospitality industry to treat your customers as guests. By guests I mean people you actually like, not that third-cousin on your mother's second husband's side that always embarrasses everyone and spilled cocktail sauce on your brand new Persian rug.

Guests are more likely than customers to become friends, and friends tend to be more loyal than customers. Therefore, if you treat your customers like guests, they are more likely to become loyal. I knew that introduction to logic class I took freshman year would pay off someday.

Never Assume

I am always amazed when there appears to be a direct correlation between my style of dress and the quality of service I receive. Either way I'm the same person with the same limits on my credit cards.

My attire generally reflects my mood, particularly on those days when I am not out playing grownup. More often than not, I'm in rock & roll mode. Translated, that means I'm wearing a bandana, T-shirt, jeans or sweats, sunglasses and probably unshaven. In other words, I look like I'm on my way to a Grateful Dead concert.

I will rarely, if ever, purchase anything at a store where I have determined that I am treated differently based on my appearance.

Assumptions are the first sign of impending disaster. The idiot-proof principle here is to never assume.

Moments of Truth

Every interaction with a customer, whether it is in person, on the telephone or through written correspondence, is a moment of truth. It is during these moments of truth that loyalty is earned.

Each moment of truth is like a magnifying glass to the eyes of your customer and every single one gets stored in the their memory bank. The more positive moments of truth you create for your customers, the more likely you are to earn their loyalty.

The fake customer service smile never cuts it during a moment of truth!!

The Great Barrier

"But that's the way we've always done it." If I had a dollar for every time I have heard that, I would be off on a yacht in the South Pacific.

TTWWADI (that's the way we've always done it) is truly the great barrier to customer loyalty...with one caveat. If the way you have always done things has created the level of customer loyalty you desire, keep it up. However, I doubt that that is the case, since if it was you probably would not be reading this book.

If you continue to do what you have always done, you will continue to get the results that you have always gotten.

Here's a real complicated concept. If doing things the way you have always done them is not creating customer loyalty, change the way you are doing things. That is one of the most potent idiot-proof principles of all-time.

Remember, the only difference between a rat and a human being running through a maze with no reward at the end is that eventually the rat will stop running. Think about it.

Voice mail: the device of choice for companies that want to offend their customers without making the effort to do so live and in person.

Ask, Listen and Act

Have you ever taken the time to ask your customers what they like or do not like about doing business with you?

If not, is it because you are a mind reader or that you know intuitively how they feel? Or is it that you don't really care what they think? If you do ask, do you use their responses to do things differently? If not, don't even bother asking. If you aren't going to use what you have learned to better serve your customer, do not waste their time or yours.

An amazing thing will happen when you ask your customers what they like and what they don't like. They will tell you! Your customer's responses will actually provide you with the road map to their loyalty. Follow your customer's directions and you will earn their loyalty. What a concept!

This is not brain surgery. Ask your customers what you can do better and when they tell you, do it! It doesn't get much more idiot-proof than that.

Listen to what your customers say as if you will be tested on it, because you probably will be!

Customer Surveys

Stop wasting your customer's time with those ridiculous satisfaction surveys and start asking them two simple questions:

1. Will you recommend us to a friend?

2. If not, why not?

No matter how they respond, thank them profusely because they are doing you a huge favor!

Customer Loyalty Initiatives

Start a customer loyalty initiative in your company. Before you begin developing your initiative, just a word of caution. Avoid the creation of a customer service committee at all costs. I don't know about you, but I'm allergic to committees. Most of them do not achieve anything more than massive coffee and donut consumption. And we have plenty of government workers available to handle those two critical tasks.

Committees tend to be a huge waste of everyone's time. An initiative, on the other hand, implies action.

This does not have to be a hugely complicated affair. Begin by soliciting input from your customers, both internal and external. Then take action on what you have learned.

By finding ways to keep customer service uppermost in the minds of everyone in your organization, you will be well on your way to creating customer loyalty.

Customer service
is invisible.
You don't see it,
but you sure
do feel it!

Trading Places

Everyone in your company should know what it's like in the trenches. By that I mean each person, from the CEO to supervisors, should periodically spend a day working on the front lines of customer service.

Inevitably, executives who do this gain greater insight into the challenges inherent in those frontline positions. In addition to earning the respect of their employees, these leaders become more likely to invest in the resources necessary for the proper training and support to develop true customer service professionals.

As an added bonus, this will do wonders for employee morale, because they will see that their bosses care enough about them to come out of the ivory towers to get firsthand knowledge of the challenges they face on a daily basis.

If you are not serving customers directly, your job is to be serving someone who is!

Internal Customers

They are typically the forgotten customers, and they are always the most important customers. Internal customers, or employees, will make or break a company. Your company's internal customers represent the foundation of your customer service. They are the cornerstones, without which loyalty is unattainable.

You can always get a sense of how a company will treat you by observing how they treat their employees. Brochures and commercials can promise you the moon, but if a company treats its frontline employees poorly, you can bet that you will be treated poorly, too. Conversely, when a company treats its employees well, you can be confident that those employees will treat you with the care, courtesy and respect you deserve.

Employee loyalty is vastly underrated, yet it is not a particularly complicated issue. Treat employees well by recognizing and praising their efforts. Let them know that what they are doing is contributing to the overall success of the company as well as making them more marketable in their own careers. Give them small, unexpected rewards for jobs well done.

I recently asked a company CEO how he personally demonstrated that he cared for his employees. He looked at me quizzically and said in an annoyed tone, "I give them a paycheck." What an idiot! It's no surprise that their turnover rate is sky high, employee morale is in the toilet and the company is in danger of going under.

According to the United States Department of Labor, the average employee turnover for 2006 was nearly twenty-five percent! How can you expect to earn customer loyalty if you don't have the loyalty of your own employees?

"You can tell the quality of management in any organization by the way you are treated by their front line staff."

Craig Farrell
Former president and CEO
Choice Hotels Canada

Exceeding Expectations

Exceeding expectations is not the daunting task it appears to be. Consumers have been beaten into submission. Most of the time they are just hoping the experience won't be too much of a hassle. In other words, they have become conditioned to expect pathetic service. Consequently, their expectations are pretty low.

As a customer, that is a sad state of affairs. On the flip side, it is a terrific opportunity for you as a service provider to distinguish yourself from the crowd of mediocrity. It provides the occasion to use your creativity in order to delight your customers. Get into the habit of doing a little something extra or unexpected.

My favorite example of someone who exceeds expectations by creatively doing a little something extra is a nurse named Bonnie. Whenever she notices that someone is having a particularly bad day, Bonnie provides them with her anti-depression kit. It comes in a little bag, complete with a note explaining each of the ingredients. Bonnie's anti-depression kit includes an eraser, so you can make all your mistakes disappear; a penny, so you will never have to say I'm broke; a marble, in case someone says you've lost all your marbles; a rubber band, to stretch yourself beyond your limits; a string, to tie things together when everything falls apart; a hug coupon and a chocolate kiss, to remind you that someone, somewhere cares about you. Do you think Bonnie exceeds people's expectations?

The idiot-proof formula for exceeding your customer's expectations is to promise much, but deliver more.

The Ultimate Creativity Formula

C=MSU,

Creativity = Make Stuff Up

Use Your Creativity!

Start using your creativity to make your own rules for how fabulously you are going to treat your customers in order to delight them with a memorable experience.

Creativity is most definitely NOT thinking out-of-the-box! Pardon the rant, but that is a stupid term that has absolutely no meaning! If it is necessary to constantly think out-of-the-box, then it's a bad box!! Throw it away, or if you want to be politically correct, recycle it.

As it applies to customer service, creativity is simply using your imagination to create an amazing experience. It is refusing to take yes for an answer in your quest to turn good into spectacular!

If you make the rules
should you
win the game?
Of course!
If you can make the
rules, you can win.
If you can win,
you should.
If you should win,
you must.
If you must win,
you will.
Are you willing to
make the rules?

Passion

Passion is more than just a persistent preoccupation with an idea that other people consider unreasonable.

People will tell you it is unreasonable to think that you can create a whole community of wildly loyal customers. Of course you can do it, but only by exploiting your passion and becoming obsessed with delivering loyalty-inducing service.

Passion will not only help you to serve more effectively, it will bring more energy, enthusiasm and creativity into your life than you ever imagined possible. And passion is contagious.

Would you rather do business with someone who exudes the fire of passion or someone who is merely doing their job? Most people view their jobs as places where they work just hard enough to avoid getting fired while getting paid just enough to avoid quitting. How pleasant is it to do business with these individuals?

Bring the passion of your excitement and enthusiasm to your customers and they will buy more from you and tell others about the experience.

Why? Because passion persuades!

Self-service: a customer service term meaning, "Do it yourself because we don't care enough about you to get off our butts and help you!"

Demonstrate Gratefulness

Thankfulness is one of the pillars of creating customer loyalty. Be genuinely grateful for your customers and you will naturally treat them with a phenomenal level of respect, caring and, dare I say, love.

Be outrageous in demonstrating your love for your customers. It is actually pretty easy to love your customers when you remember that they are the people paying for your kids' education so that you don't have to suffer from mal-tuition. They are also paying your mortgage and sponsoring your early retirement.

It is not enough to merely feel appreciation and love for your customers. You must constantly find little ways to *demonstrate your love and appreciation to them.*

Never underestimate the power of a thoughtful thank you. How would it affect your business if your customers knew that you loved and appreciated them? What if they felt great about it and went out and told lots of other people how wonderful you are? Do the math.

When you realize how hard customers are to come by, it's a no-brainer that you have to do everything in your power to make them feel appreciated.

Remember, small acts of kindness and appreciation can make a huge difference. They take only a few seconds, yet can help create lifelong customers. Your customers will take their business where they feel appreciated!

It all comes back to the fact that loyalty is an emotion, and love and appreciation are incredibly powerful emotions. What can you do today to genuinely demonstrate love and appreciation for your customers?

Make every day customer appreciation day!

Attitude

Every self-help guru in the world spews sermons about attitude and every super-achiever touts the impact of having a positive attitude. Since success tends to leave clues, perhaps this is an area worth exploring.

As a rule of thumb, positive attitudes yield positive results. Lousy attitudes yield lousy results. Again, not rocket science. Customer service is an attitude, not a department. And there is a huge difference between having a positive attitude and simply having attitude.

Most of the places I go I feel like the customer service representatives have *attitude*. Even though I'm preparing to fork over my hard earned money, it feels like they think they are doing me some huge favor. In reality, I am doing them a favor by helping to put food on their tables.

Much like Disney employees are in character when they greet guests at their theme parks, you are on stage whenever you are dealing with customers. Your customers are quickly making judgments about whether or not they want to do business with you based on your attitude.

Your attitude is reflected through your interactions with your customers and is an indication of your feelings toward them. Again, put yourself in your customer's shoes. Would you rather do business with people who have a positive attitude or those who simply have attitude?

If you can't be upbeat and positive you should probably find a new line of work because without a positive attitude you will fail miserably in the people business.

Joe's Guarantee

A positive attitude may not solve all your problems, but it will annoy enough people to make it worth the effort.

The Fun Factor

Learn to put the 'fun' back in dysfunctional. We all know that the workplace is dysfunctional under the best of circumstances, so why not just admit it and use it to your advantage.

Cyndi Lauper wrote a delightfully memorable song titled *Girls Just Wanna Have Fun.* Speaking on behalf of the rest of our species, boys wanna have fun, too! Your customers are all boys and girls. Therefore, they wanna have fun. What are you doing to make it fun?

Create a revolving director of mirth, a different employee each month who is responsible for bringing some fun into the workplace. Make it an organization-wide initiative. Institute a fun suggestion box. Involve your customers, too. They will absolutely love it.

Although you probably already have someone unofficially handling this task, you could also designate an interoffice coordination clerk. That's the person who is responsible for making and distributing copies of the latest cartoons and comics. They are going to circulate anyway, so why not make it a company-sanctioned activity that is done openly on a regular basis.

Fun is contagious. If your employees are having fun, it will rub off on your customers. And if your customers perceive doing business with you to be fun, they will look for more opportunities to visit you and they will tell other people about the experience.

Most businesses are staffed by the terminally adult, and fun is the best antidote to terminal adulthood. When you endorse the child-like quality of fun and actively encourage employees to enjoy themselves, you will draw a crowd in no time.

Create opportunities for your internal customers to lighten up and have fun! A major benefit of this is that when people are having fun they tend to be more productive.

Work, like life, is meant to be enjoyed and not merely endured. And you just might be surprised at how it positively affects your bottom line.

If fun is not a priority on your daily agenda, then you are an idiot!

If you always do fun things there will always be plenty of fun things to do!

The Power of Humor

Humor is the great equalizer. When you make someone laugh, you make them feel good. When they feel good around you, they tend to feel good about you. When they feel good about you, they want to do business with you.

Southwest Airlines is a classic example of a company that understands the importance of humor in creating customer loyalty. They are one of the few companies I have encountered that asks you to describe your sense of humor on their job application.

People want to work at Southwest Airlines because it's fun and they will get to laugh a lot on the job. They get treated well, have a good time and enjoy their jobs. While they are getting treated so well and having such a good time, these employees treat the customers great and make us laugh. When they make us laugh we feel good. And we keep doing business with people who make us feel good. Is it any wonder that for the last twenty years they have had the lowest number of passenger complaints in the industry?

Consequently, Southwest Airlines has created tremendous customer loyalty and is successful in an industry where profitability is harder to come by than a politician who knows right from wrong.

Following are two great examples of humor that caught my attention. First, a sign on the tip jar in a little coffee shop said, "If you fear change, leave it here!" When I read that I laughed so hard I nearly dropped my coffee.

The next one was a sign on the side of a plumber's truck that read, "A flush always beats a full house." Without knowing anything else about them, it made me feel like they were a company that I could do business with.

If your customers associate chuckles and laughter with you, that creates a positive impression of your company in their minds. That positive impression increases the likelihood that they will want to do more business with you and tell others about their experience.

Important note: Do NOT tell jokes to your customers! You do not do it well, no matter what your spouse and kids tell you. Just learn to look at the lighter side of life. This will make your daily experiences much more enjoyable, while bringing a smile to the faces of the people you encounter.

It's truly idiot-proof. We want to deal with people who inspire positive feelings in us, and there is no more pleasurable feeling than laughter. In other words, humor is a secret weapon for creating customer loyalty.

"If we couldn't laugh we would all go insane."

Jimmy Buffet

Create a Community of Crazed Loyalists

Do something to make your customers feel like they are part of a community when they use your product or service. That will give them another reason to become insanely true to your brand.

A company in my hometown is a classic example of an organization that has created a community of crazed loyalists. That company is Harley-Davidson.

Harley has developed an incredibly loyal customer base not only for their motorcycles, but for their clothing and accessories as well. They have even introduced their own line of beef jerky, calling it 'fuel for the wide open road'. Do they know their customers or what?

Harley-Davidson is more than just a company...they are both a mindset and a happening. Why else would tens of thousands of crazed HOG (Harley Owners Group) loyalists from all over the world invade Milwaukee every time Harley celebrates an anniversary? Anniversary parties don't get any bigger or better than the ones Harley puts on. Harley further solidifies their relationship with an intensely loyal community through these events.

What are you currently doing to inspire that type of crazed loyalty to your brand?

Ignore the Competition!

Stop paying attention to your competition, because in all likelihood their customer service sucks. Therefore, if you compare yourself to them it is easy to settle for mediocrity, which is only a small step up the ladder from sucking. Mediocrity will still outperform the majority of your industry, but it most assuredly will not inspire customer loyalty!

If you really want to stand out from the crowd, pay attention to Disney. They have created a model for service excellence that is unparalleled, and the principles they embrace are universal.

How much customer loyalty could you create if your service culture mirrored Disney's?

"The painter will produce mediocre pictures if he is inspired by the work of other painters."

Leonardo da Vinci

The Loyalty Connection

Your ability to create customer loyalty is directly related to your ability to connect with people, or establish rapport. Rapport is simply communicating with another person in a manner that allows them to feel connected to you. It is a sense of commonality or alignment.

When you create rapport with your customers they will feel good when they are around you. When they feel good around you, they will feel good about you. When they feel good about you, they are much more likely to become loyal than if they feel indifferent toward you.

The best and quickest way to create rapport is to become a fantastic listener. The key is to take the attention off of you and put it on your customer. When you listen you make the other person the star. Listening also gives you the opportunity to learn as much as possible about your customer's wants and needs.

Listening is more than merely waiting for your turn to speak. It is temporarily suspending your own agenda to focus intently on your customer. There is nothing more flattering than the laser beam-like undivided attention of another person.

The greatest gift that you can give to another person is to be one hundred percent present in their presence. That is the essence of listening. And a good listener is not only popular everywhere, but eventually they know something.

The idiot-proof truth is that we prefer doing business with people we like and trust. In other words, people with whom we feel a connection. That is the loyalty connection.

The World's Shortest Communication Seminar

Shut up and listen!

Duh!

The Silver Tongue Rule

Communicate with each individual you encounter as if you have to spend the rest of your life with that person in very close quarters.

The Fallacy of Quality

If quality determines customer loyalty, how can you possibly explain Domino's Pizza?!?!?

How do they command such amazing customer loyalty when their product is so lousy? It's really quite simple. They make people feel good about doing business with them.

See if this sounds familiar. It's the end of the workday. Before you go home you have to stop and pay eight dollars a gallon for gas, pick up tofu, wheat germ and broccoli at the grocery store, stop at the dry cleaner and then pick little Johnny up from soccer practice.

What did you forget? Oh, no...you begin to lament what a terrible parent you are because you forgot about dinner for the family. And then you stop and reframe the scenario.

OK, right before you stop at the dry cleaners you'll call Domino's. Since it takes approximately twenty-seven minutes to pick up both the dry cleaning and little Johnny and then drive home, you'll arrive just about the time the delivery person brings your pizza. And maybe you're not such a bad parent after all since you really can put a lukewarm meal on the dinner table.

Even though Domino's hasn't had their "thirty minutes or it's free" guarantee for a number of years, most people still associate Domino's with rapid delivery. They have created the feeling that you can depend on them when you are in a time crunch.

I am certainly not suggesting that you should try to get by with less than great quality. I assume that your product or service is first-rate. If it's not, you don't deserve customer loyalty. But, as Domino's has clearly demonstrated, shoddy quality is not always a deal breaker.

If quality determines customer loyalty, how can you possibly explain Domino's Pizza?

Pathetic Policies

Policies are the sworn enemies of customer loyalty. In fact, they are usually loyalty assassins. I have rarely seen a policy that was written to protect the customer. In fact, most of the policies that I have read appear to serve no real purpose other than to alienate the customer. That may not be the intent, but it is most often the result.

Policies that are designed to protect only the company cause tremendous resentment among customers. Although it wasn't clearly spelled out earlier, resentment is not one of the defining characteristics of customer loyalty.

What is the first thing that goes through your mind when someone tells you "Our company policy is...?" If you are like most people that I have asked, when you hear those four words you are relatively certain that you are going to get the raw end of the deal. Whenever an employee refers to their company policies, what I really hear is, "we care so little about our customers that we created these inane rules to ensure that we don't have to go out of our way to make you happy. After all, we're in business to make money for ourselves and you are just a necessary evil in the process."

If you must write a customer service policy, write it from the customer's perspective. No ifs, ands or buts.

Company policy: the corporate equivalent of your parents saying, "Because I said so!"

The Ultimate Risk Reversal Guarantee

What guarantees do you offer to your customers? A guarantee is nothing more than your commitment that something will be performed in a specified manner. Yes, I did slip in the big C word—commitment. I realize that word scares a lot of people, particularly the males of our species. However, it is a necessary ingredient in the customer loyalty equation.

Your customers deserve some assurance that if something goes wrong, you will make it right. If you can't, or are not willing to, guarantee the caliber of your product or service then you do not deserve their loyalty. It also means that you don't believe what you are offering is first-rate quality.

One great way to assure your customers of your commitment is to offer the ultimate risk reversal guarantee. Never let your customers feel like it is a risk to do business with you. If you stand behind the quality you provide, it's easy to offer a 'no-questions-asked, you-be-the-judge money back guarantee'.

The ultimate risk reversal guarantee makes a powerful statement to your customers. It sends the message that you care so much about their business that you are willing to do whatever it takes to delight them. Do you think they will share that with other people?

Guarantee your customers that you will do exactly what you say you are going to do, when you say you are going to do it, the way you promised to do it. Then, tell the world about this commitment to your customers. It's another idiot-proof way of setting yourself apart from the competition.

Loyalty is earned by dazzling one person at a time.

Complaints and Service Recovery

One of the fastest and surest ways to assess your company's commitment to excellence in customer service is the manner in which you handle complaints.

People want their complaints handled immediately, if not sooner. Promptness counts. We know that if complaints are resolved at the time they are lodged, and the customer feels good about how the situation was handled, they are likely to both keep coming back and praise you when they tell others how you handled the matter. With that in mind, look for ways to do a little something extra for the customer in the process.

Learn to reframe complaints. Think of them as opportunities to improve the level of service you are delivering, since you are learning what your customer thinks you are doing poorly. Additionally, when customers complain they are giving you a chance to earn their loyalty with a dazzling recovery.

Only a very small percentage of customers with complaints will tell you, so they are actually doing you a valuable service. Whether complaining customers become loyal depends on your recovery. If you thrill them with the recovery, they will likely forget about the problem. When you make things right in the eyes of your customer, the recovery becomes the focal point of the story that your customer shares with other people.

Here's a six-step system for stellar service recovery:

1. Thank the customer for alerting you to the problem.

2. Apologize sincerely for the inconvenience.

3. Fix the problem and resolve the matter.

4. Thank the customer for the opportunity to make things right.

5. Do a little something extra.

6. Thank the customer again.

When you are handling complaints, keep in mind what the customer does not want to hear. They don't want to hear excuses about why your company screwed up. Customers do not care who is to blame, they are not interested in hearing about your staffing shortage and they couldn't care less about your computer problems!

Remember that an upset customer can do extensive damage to your company's reputation, and they rarely hesitate to do so. It is estimated that upset customers tell between eight and twelve people about their negative experiences. Consequently, spending a few extra dollars to make them happy is almost always worth the effort and expense.

PITA Customers

You know who they are. I call them the PITA customers. PITA is an acronym for Pain In The...Arm.

These people are the chronic complainers who are never happy with anything. Whatever you do or say is always wrong. You could give them a lifetime supply of your product or service for free and they would still find something to whine about.

The PITA people often take up so much of your time and energy that they actually end up costing you money, in addition to the excessive aggravation that you might inadvertently take out on one of your loyal customers.

Eventually, you need to take a stand with the PITA people. Don't even worry about them bad-mouthing you. Everyone they know already realizes they are chronic complainers and nobody even listens to them anymore. And if they do listen, they're as likely as not to give you their business as a reward for putting up with them as long as you did.

Here is the best way I know to deal with the chronic PITA customer. I hate the idea of using scripts, but this is the exception to that rule:

"Mr. Grumbleton, our only goal is to make you happy. We have done everything we possibly can and you still appear extremely upset. Maybe it would be best if we help you find someone else to work with that can better meet your needs."

Typically, one of two things will then happen. Either they will stop complaining while continuing to come back or they will go away and you won't have to deal with them anymore. Either way, you win. I realize you never want to lose a customer, but sometimes you've got to know when to cut your losses when dealing with the PITAs of the world.

And you thought Pita was just a bread that tastes good with humus.

Thirty-three: the percent your profits will increase if you get rid of the ten percent of your customers who cause ninety percent of your headaches.

Raising the Bar

The mindset for providing fabulous service is one of consistently raising the bar of excellence. Don't panic. This isn't some grandiose plan that requires a comprehensive overhaul of everything that you are currently doing.

Raising the bar simply means that you focus on elevating your level of service one percent every day. By improving one percent each day you will double your effectiveness in only seventy days.

What a concept! You can be twice as good at anything in only ten weeks by improving one measly percent each day.

Do you reckon your customer loyalty would increase exponentially if your service levels were twice as good as the are right now?

What is Customer Loyalty?

Just checking to see if you have been paying attention. You already know that customer loyalty is a **feeling** that people have about doing business with you.

Remember, you can't afford the luxury of having merely satisfied customers because they will leave you in a heartbeat for a better deal. Loyal customers, on the other hand, are like a motivated sales force that you don't even have to pay. They actually pay you for the opportunity to be walking, talking billboards for your company! How cool is that?

Customer Loyalty from A-D

Since I didn't give you the A-Z guide to customer loyalty, the least I can do is provide the A-D version.

To earn customer loyalty all you need to do is go

> **A**bove and
> **B**eyond the
> **C**all of
> **D**uty

The World's Shortest Customer Loyalty Seminar

1. Be nice.
2. Be helpful
3. Amplify these two principles by using your creativity in a manner that makes your customers say WOW!

Attempt the impossible in order to achieve the incredible!

Jamaica has a bobsled team— what exactly is it that you can't do?

The World's Shortest Motivational Seminar

1. Decide
2. Do

Duh!

Just Do It

Customer loyalty will be created as a result of the actions you take on behalf of your customers. The ultimate success of your business will unfold based on the implementation of these idiot-proof actions. Although you can't necessarily control the outcome, you do have total control over your actions.

Your rewards will come not from your knowledge about customer loyalty, but from what you do with what you know. If you have gotten this far, you already know everything you need to know about earning customer loyalty. What you do with it is up to you.

Remember these words from Casey Stengel, "They say it can't be done, but that don't always work."

And one last thing…it's only idiot-proof if you actually do it!

About the Author

Joe Heuer is a wildly entertaining speaker known for his uniquely humorous style and idiot-proof approach to customer service, motivation and life in general. He has been called the "Dr. Phil" of customer service, although his wife insists that he is an idiot savant for his uncanny recall of obscure rock & roll lyrics.

Joe is the author of several books and is known internationally as a humorist for his popular Daffynitions.

Joe and his wife, Lisa, along with their amazing twin daughters, reside in suburban Milwaukee, Wisconsin.

If you're looking for a dynamic and fun speaker, or to order any of Joe Heuer's books and products, please contact:

JoeSpeaks!

2435 West Greenwood Road
Glendale, Wisconsin 53209

800.492.3548
414.247.0936

joespeaks.com
iknowitsonlyrockandroll.com
daffynitions.com

Thank you!

The band has left the building.